Would you like to find a dinosaur? You cannot find a real dinosaur. All the dinosaurs are gone from the earth.

But, we can find clues the dinosaurs left. We can learn about dinosaurs from these clues.

These are dinosaur footprints.
The prints were left in mud. The
mud turned to rock. The
footprints are very big. So, we
know that some dinosaurs were
very big.

These are bones from
dinosaurs. The bones turned to
rock. We learn about the
bodies of dinosaurs from bones
like these.

These are dinosaur eggs that
have turned to rocks! This shows
us that some dinosaurs laid eggs.

This is the skin of a baby
dinosaur. It was still inside one
of the eggs. It shows us that
some dinosaurs had rough skin.

We think some dinosaurs looked like this. We guess this from the clues we find.

Sue Hendrickson found some dinosaur bones. When the bones were put together, they made the biggest T. rex ever found. The dinosaur was named Sue, after its finder. Maybe some day you will find a dinosaur and it will be named after you!